Mountain

A collection of Haiku and Senryu poems

by

Scott P Mitchell

Sunwater Publications

Published by Sunwater Publications
PO Box 3155
Pottsville NSW 2489

© Copyright Scott P Mitchell 2020
ISBN 978-0-6489547-0-5

This book is copyright. Apart from any fair dealing for the purpose of private study, research, criticism or review, as permitted under the Copyright Act, no part may be reproduced by any process without written permission of the author.

All rights reserved
First published as a Sunwater publishing 2020

Cover photography: Scott P Mitchell
(The view from my window)

This book is dedicated to my daughter
Mirabai
whose light is the envy of the sun.

Preface

I clearly remember writing my first Haiku. My brother and I were sharing a house at the turn of the millenia. Our front garden had a white picket fence that accommodated an overgrown lavender bush, some kangaroo paws and an assortment of Australian wild flowers. It had been a particularly cold winter and I awoke one morning to sit on my verandah with a morning coffee. The sun was bright and warm, clear blue skies, bees were frantic on the budding lavender and wildflowers. It was the quintessential spring morning after a long winter. I was engulfed by the moment and the jubilance of it's arrival. From this experience came the poem...

spring
   now's there's red
      where there wasn't any

Being a musician and songwriter I had been writing in journals and crafting poems for many years. I had a collection of poetry books which included the works of various Haiku poets. Around this time I found myself drawn to minimalism in art and word. This was inspired by the painter Mark Rothko after attending an exhibition at the West Australian Art Gallery. To this day I have never been so affected by art as upon the viewing of his work. Somehow it translated to poetry for me and the logical direction was to the Haiku and Senryu styles. I wrote solely for myself as a kind of meditation, an immersion into the presence of being. It has never been an ambitious activity. As Jeff Buckley once said "The process is the goal"...as is with Haiku.

During one of my editing sessions it occured to me that I had ammassed quite a collection. I sent a selection to a good friend in Norway who recommended compiling them into a book. To confirm their validity I sent another basket of poems to a respected Haiku Journal. When 'pistachios' was selected to be printed in the spring journal, I received the confirmation that I was looking for to publish my work.

These poems span over a period of twenty years. Like all crafts I have learnt and studied the masters but have always determined my own style. After all I am an Australian living on this island continent and can't help but be influenced by my culture and environment. These poems are me, as I am, here and now.

bush walk
looking for the waterfall
we spot a koala

surfing alone
dorsal fin
phew!...just a dolphin

by the riverside
possessing a dead tree
murder of crows

tropical rain

a ring of mushrooms

    we both avoid entering

moon to the left   sun to the right
        w   i   d   e
    o p e n
        r
        o
        a
        d

sweeping up the sound
of shattered glass...
my favourite coffee cup

a gap in the clouds
    moonlight dimming
        the lightening

making tea upstairs
the mood
in her footsteps

turning off my computer
listening
to thunder

shadow on the ground
of a lizard
on the roof

gentle rain
shades the intervals
of a leaking faucet

slowly   placing the phone
on the kitchen table...
second suicide in six months

between the art studio
and music room
the kitchen is quiet

washing the dishes loudly-
    to make a point

toilet wall...
an old atlas picture
daddy longlegs   crosses the Himalayas

morning rain
   picking mushrooms
      only the golden tops...

days later
the wiltered wedding rose's
lingering perfume

during the 'pandemic'
   yellow butterflies
      in afternoon sun

low tide
the moon inside
a dead fish eye

to the floor
I drop the last chocolate...
    3 second rule

we both turn
to look at each other
tiger snake

my new bamboo flute-
even bum notes
have a place   in eternity

mimicking the wind outside
my daughters coloring in...

winter...
negotiating a slippery leaf
snail in the rain

burying the

tawny frog mouth

   ants track the beak

lotus pond...
the python's
pink mouth

while reading
vacuuming around my feet
    thoughts of divorce....

hiding under the
red corduroy beanbag:
my Bob Dylan T-shirt

twilight moon
with the sky
all to itself

facing off...
three legged dog
one legged seagull

the second eagle

stealing

the first eagles fish

the dying seabird's
flickering eye...
    waves rolling in

while listening to the Doors first album
"roll one up!"

years later...
my first sitar
broken   in the pawnshop

lipstick on yellow teeth
the hairdresser
cuts my fringe

keeping me awake-
split toenail
bedsheets

with words about the silence   breaking the silence

the street performers eyes
sombre
as the sound of his cello

through the grapevine
    she burnt all his flutes...
        and our reunion

pinching me
she says
"are you awake?"

                    top
                the
            reach
            I
        mountain
        the
climbing

staring at my sitar

like lovers

after an argument

spring
    now's there's red
        where there wasn't any

before the storm
clouds   like feathers

morning sun
silhouettes of tombstones
the crow's hark

mountain peak
peeks it peak
over the clouds

my reading chair
infested with fleas-
the cat licks it's ass

while doodling
an accidental   perfect circle

mountain   mountain

         valley

but for three
sealed pistachios
    the empty bowl...

on my bookshelf
'Tropic of Cancer'
seventeen years overdue...

winter
r　　a　　i　　n　　i　　n　　g
warm　　　cozy　　　bed

still pond
sky cloud and sunshine
shimmer   in a breathe of wind

fish in beak
flying back to the nest
thunder

glass cage
the death adder
threatening no one

bush turkey
gobbles
at a step in his direction

holding up traffic
the hare krishna
guides a snake   across the road

faint crackle of dragonfly wings
devouring prey
the huntsman spider

monsoon rains-
nudging the lotus
the big   golden koi

if silence whispered...
the sho*
    I covet

*The sho is a reed flute consisting of 17 slender bamboo pipes originating from Japan.

after the rains
a cluster of
wild   spiky mushrooms

night
   above the jungle drone
      silence of stars

tiny silverfish on my page
smaller than
the g of morning

lazy afternoon
sunlight
in a bowl of lemons

night sky
oblique satellites
m   o   a   s t
    o   m   t i   a
o n   u n   n   r   s

dreaming of a forest fire
my wifes coughing
wakes me up...

through a glass of water
　outside
　　is upside down

a giant eagle
spiralling
in the updraft

every morning-

the little jetty

where the pelicans meet

looking down

I notice I'm sitting

as my grandfather used to

pause...
a deep conversation
    flickering candle flame

coffee bruschetta
mandarin caramel slice
chicken potato wine chocolate

white circle

crows eye

peering through the back door

after moving house
the books on the bookshelf
are all wrong

daughter

"who was the first person on the earth?"

    I look out to sea...

ceremony...
in a glass bottle
    the medicine

drinking from the cup
with a single gulp
    it's my turn next

the shamans song
guides the journey
to where I'm afraid to go...

the fading rainbow...
fiddling with phone camera

the books I donated

to the old bookstore-

      gathering the shops dust...

forest
the only straight lines
shafts   of morning sun

my old haiku book—
flakes of ganja
wedged in the spine

by the fire
cat whiskers
tickle my toes

cracking the morning sand
like crème brûlée-
    a walk on the beach

my car   and a plane-
head on collision
      in the shadows

stick insect
stretching his back leg
    morning coffee

summer rain...
releasing the perfume
of eucalyptus trees

bushfire skies...
orange sunshine
touches her cheek

waking
morning bird
singing in the dawn

compost pile-
   a yellow eyed crow
      picks at a banana skin

the red sky

behind my eyelids

as I   look into the sun

sunlit bathroom tiles-
random hair
spelling the word   boobs

steam from my coffee cup
    incense smoke
        commingle in morning light...

perched for prey
the python   as still
as the wall it's on

morning river
drawing the ocean into itself...
pelicans on the bank

city
walking in rhythm
to the car alarm

meditating...
fly buzzing 'round my head
like a Jackson Pollock painting

resting on the
outdoor chessboard
    black and white bird

         f

         a

         l

         l

         i

         n

         g

      r   o

   d   p

      o f

        rain

hot summer night
I turn the pillow over
   for the cool side

birds in V formation
a plane
heading in the same direction

6.00am   now I get up
when I used to go to bed
fatherhood...

sardonic laughter
of a drunkard...
echoing in the wind

listening to
old jazz...
'So What'

after the rain
      looking for worms
a pigeon toed magpie

thistle seed
flying in the breeze
and out to sea

swerving to miss
a rainbow lorikeet...
        rearview mirror   feathers

autumn-
that dip in the mountains
where the sun sets...

drought
the creek I swim in
dust on my feet

my forest home
not a cherry blossom
in sight

www.ingramcontent.com/pod-product-compliance
Lightning Source LLC
Chambersburg PA
CBHW070310010526
44107CB00056B/2549